W9-DEW-384

AMENDMENTS TO THE UNITED STATES CONSTITUTION
THE BILL OF RIGHTS

RIGHTS RETAINED
BY THE PEOPLE

KATHY FURGANG

rosen publishing's
**rosen
central®**

New York

To Caleb and Ben

Published in 2011 by The Rosen Publishing Group, Inc.
29 East 21st Street, New York, NY 10010

First Edition

Library of Congress Cataloging-in-Publication Data

Furgang, Kathy.
The Ninth Amendment: rights retained by the people / Kathy Furgang. — 1st ed.
    p. cm. — (Amendments to the United States Constitution: the Bill of Rights)
Includes bibliographical references and index.
ISBN 978-1-4488-1264-6 (library binding)
ISBN 978-1-4488-2310-9 (pbk.)
ISBN 978-1-4488-2316-1 (6-pack)
1. United States. Constitution. 9th Amendment—Juvenile literature. 2. Civil rights—United States—Juvenile literature. 3. Constitutional law—United States—Juvenile literature. I. Title.
KF45589th .F87 2011
342.7308'5—dc22

2010020091

Manufactured in the United States of America

CPSIA Compliance Information: Batch #W11YA: For further information, contact Rosen Publishing, New York, New York, at 1-800-237-9932.

On the cover: Abortion rights supporters and opponents express their differing viewpoints before the Supreme Court building in Washington, D.C. Abortion rights are among the "privacy rights" some people argue are covered by the Ninth Amendment.

CONTENTS

INTRODUCTION

Americans have specific rights and freedoms, and they are taken very seriously by courts and citizens alike. When the country was founded in the late 1700s following the American Revolution, the U.S. Constitution was written to spell out the fundamental principles that would govern the new nation. The specific rights of American citizens were laid out in the Bill of Rights, which are the first ten amendments, or revisions, to the Constitution. For example, as part of the Bill of Rights, the right to privacy is guaranteed under the Ninth Amendment.

However, when reading the text of the Ninth Amendment, one doesn't come across any references to privacy. In fact, the right to privacy

Over time, Supreme Court interpretations of the Ninth Amendment have resulted in certain guarantees to the individual's right to privacy. Many people feel this includes freedom from unwarranted wiretaps or other forms of electronic eavesdropping. However, the text of the amendment does not actually mention the word "privacy."

is not specified anywhere in the entire Bill of Rights or any of the seventeen other amendments to the Constitution that were ratified in later years. That's because the Ninth Amendment is worded in such a way that it guarantees a range of citizen rights without having to specifically name each and every one of them. It is written in this vague, open-ended way in order to make sure that individual rights are not denied even though they are not specifically named. The text of the amendment states, "The enumeration in the Constitution, of certain rights, shall not be construed to deny or disparage others retained by the people."

When the Bill of Rights was first drafted, it was feared that if each and every right of the individual was not clearly spelled out, people might be denied that right. Yet there are simply too many such rights to name. So the catchall wording of the Ninth Amendment was designed to guarantee the basic rights of the individual without inadvertently limiting or curtailing them by leaving them out of an itemized list.

As a result, this amendment is one of the hardest to interpret and enforce. But over the years, the work of the Supreme Court has helped spell out and solidify some of these basic rights. In fact, the Ninth Amendment has proved to be an extremely valuable way to protect the rights of some of the most vulnerable Americans in some of the most difficult situations.

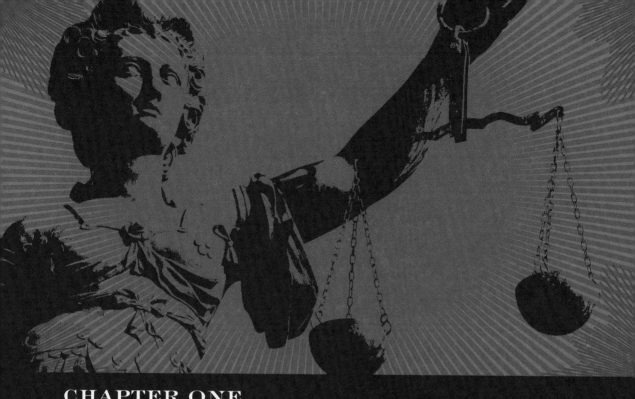

CHAPTER ONE

THE HISTORY OF THE NINTH AMENDMENT

What are some of our guaranteed rights as Americans? Perhaps the most familiar and cherished are the freedom of speech, religion, the press, assembly, and petition. American citizens also have the right to bear arms and the right to a fair trial. All of these privileges are spelled out in the Bill of Rights, the first ten amendments to the U.S. Constitution.

State vs. Federal Powers

The history of the Bill of Rights goes back as far as the history of the United States itself. After the conclusion of the Revolutionary War

In 1777, the Articles of Confederation provided a blueprint for how the state and federal governments would be structured and operated. This document granted most of the new country's governing powers to the state governments.

with Great Britain, the thirteen former colonies emerged as an independent nation. In 1783, the thirteen states completed the Articles of Confederation, which was a blueprint for how the federal and state governments would work. This document gave most of the new country's powers to the states, rather than the federal government.

The separation of state and federal powers was important to the newly founded nation. Americans were still haunted by the tyranny of the British government in the years leading up to the Revolution and wanted to prevent a similar abuse of power by a strong central government. But it soon became apparent that the federal government had too little power to be effective under the Articles of Confederation. For example, there was no executive or judicial branch of government (a president or Supreme Court). The federal government also had no power to collect taxes, regulate commerce between the states, or raise and fund an army.

In an attempt to strengthen the federal government, the U.S. Constitution was adopted by the states in 1788. This provided the federal framework we know today, with an executive, legislative (Congress), and judicial branch.

The Fight to Name the Rights of the People

Drafting and agreeing upon all of the rights and procedures contained within the U.S. Constitution was not an easy task. The gathering of leaders from each state at the Constitutional Convention in Philadelphia in 1787 proved to be a major undertaking. It was especially challenging for a young country still trying to define the relationship between the states and the federal government and between the people and the government. So why did the convention delegates not bother to include a list of "people's rights" in the 1787 Constitution? Not everyone agreed that a specific listing of citizens' rights was necessary.

The people who supported the Constitution and the new powers it gave to the federal government became known as Federalists. The people who opposed the federal government's increased role and influence—and therefore opposed much of the Constitution itself—became known as

This assembly room of Independence Hall, in Philadelphia, Pennsylvania, is where the Declaration of Independence and the Constitution were drafted, debated, and signed.

Anti-Federalists. It was the Federalists who did not think that a detailed listing of the rights of the citizens was necessary. However, the Anti-Federalists fought for these rights to be spelled out. George Mason, an Anti-Federalist from Virginia, refused to sign the Constitution because it did not include a "bill of rights" for the American people. Patrick Henry, also from Virginia, agreed. He argued that if the Constitution states that the people reserve their unalienable rights, then it must detail and list exactly what those rights are.

Federalist Theodore Sedgwick from Massachusetts joked that it is not necessary for Congress to have "declared that a man should have a right to wear his hat if he pleased; that he might get up when he pleased, and to go to bed when he thought proper." James Wilson from Pennsylvania had a similar attitude. He mused, "Enumerate all the rights of men! I am sure, sir, that no gentleman would have attempted such a thing. To every suggestion concerning a bill of rights, the citizens of the United States may always say, 'We reserve the right to do what we please!'" (as quoted in Philip Klinkner's *American Heritage History of the Bill of Rights*).

The argument over the rights of the people was just one of many passionate debates at the Constitutional Convention. Finally, however, compromises were made, agreements were reached, and the document was signed on September 17, 1787. It did not include a bill of rights for Americans. Anti-Federalists got to work right away to raise the public's awareness that citizens' specific rights were not included in the document and therefore not guaranteed by law. This campaign worked.

The Ratification Process

Even after the Bill of Rights was drafted, it took years to get the document ratified, or signed into law. Three-fourths of the states needed to sign the bill to make it part of the Constitution and make it the law of the land. It was not until 1791 that enough signatures were obtained to ratify the bill. Connecticut, Georgia, and Massachusetts never signed the Bill of Rights, but it was nevertheless passed by the other eleven states of the Union.

The process started with New Jersey signing the Bill of Rights on November 20, 1789. It finally ended on December 15, 1791, when Virginia provided the last needed signature to adopt the amendments into law. The chart below shows the dates that each state ratified the Bill of Rights.

STATE	DATE OF RATIFICATION
New Jersey	November 20, 1789
Maryland	December 19, 1789
North Carolina	December 22, 1789
South Carolina	January 19, 1790
New Hampshire	January 25, 1790
Delaware	January 28, 1790
New York	February 24, 1790
Pennsylvania	March 10, 1790
Rhode Island	June 7, 1790
Vermont	November 3, 1791
Virginia	December 15, 1791

Only two years later, enough public and political consensus had been built to introduce the ten amendments that became known as the Bill of Rights. These were ratified and went into effect in 1791.

Protecting Rights Without Naming Them

It was James Madison who drafted the Bill of Rights. He was a lawyer from Virginia who went on to become the country's fourth president. The process of debating and drafting the Bill of Rights was long and difficult. Federalists and Anti-Federalists had fierce debates about what the rights should actually be and how the ten amendments should be worded.

The Bill of Rights is still an important part of our lives today. These citizens are viewing New Jersey's original manuscript copy of the Bill of Rights on display in the state capitol building in Trenton.

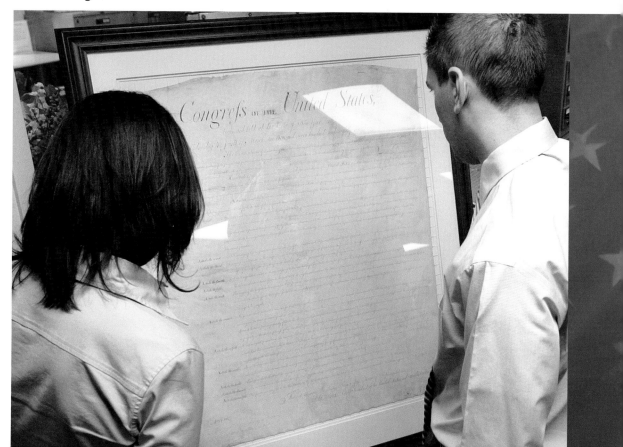

Many Federalists feared that listing the specific rights belonging to American citizens would mean that they were only entitled to those rights and no others. Basic and important rights long enjoyed by citizens might be lost simply because they had not been specifically mentioned in the Bill of Rights.

This is why the Ninth Amendment is so important. It put the minds of many skeptics at ease. The amendment specifically states that the rights mentioned in the other nine amendments are not the only rights to which Americans are entitled. Those liberties specifically mentioned in the Bill of Rights are referred to as enumerated, which means they're numbered, named, and specified. Yet the Ninth Amendment defends individual rights that are unenumerated. These are rights that are not named or specified in the Constitution or the other amendments of the Bill of Rights.

CHAPTER TWO

EARLY TESTS OF THE NINTH AMENDMENT

E ven though the Ninth Amendment was designed to help protect Americans' rights, many people—including judges, legislators, and politicians—were confused by it. If the individual's rights were not mentioned directly, how would one know exactly what these rights were? And who would decide what is and isn't a constitutionally protected right?

Following the ratification of the Bill of Rights, it would be more than one hundred years before the Ninth Amendment was first tested by the American justice system. Many of the courts that were charged with deciding issues of people's rights did not think the amendment was strong enough to withstand scrutiny.

Instead of turning to the Ninth Amendment to help settle rights disputes, the courts turned to clauses in the Fifth and Fourteenth amendments that mentioned due process, or fair treatment under the law. Over time, these amendments came to ensure that citizens would be treated fairly and equally, without regard to wealth, status, gender, ethnicity, or race. Any case centering upon an individual's rights tended to cite the Fifth Amendment and Fourteenth Amendment for legal support. The Ninth Amendment was seen as too vague to provide any useful or meaningful guidelines for deciding whether or not an individual's constitutional rights had been violated.

The Role of the Supreme Court

Whenever there is a question about the violation or interpretation of a certain law in the United States, the judicial branch of the federal government plays an important role in answering the question or settling the dispute. The Supreme Court is the highest court in the country. Each state also has a Supreme Court to deal with state issues.

The federal Supreme Court is led by a chief justice and eight other justices (judges). Each of these are nominated by the U.S. president and approved by a majority vote of the Senate. Once

The federal Supreme Court Building in Washington, D.C., is where the U.S. Supreme Court hears legal arguments, interprets the Constitution, and decides legal matters in some of the nation's most important and compelling cases.

a person is nominated and approved as a Supreme Court justice, he or she can retain that position for life. When the justice wishes to retire, the nomination and approval process is repeated to choose a new justice to fill the empty space on the bench.

The Supreme Court justices are highly respected and experienced individuals, most of whom were once judges who made many difficult decisions about the law during their pre-Supreme Court careers. States, corporations, and ordinary citizens turn to them for guidance and decisions on complicated and difficult questions regarding fundamental rights. Deceptively simple questions such as "Is education a right?" or "Is health care a right?" are actually enormously difficult and complex issues with far-reaching consequences.

Americans rely on the Supreme Court to make these decisions for them. The Supreme Court has decided many legal cases that have, with the help of the Ninth Amendment, guaranteed certain rights for women, homosexuals, and the terminally ill, among many other groups whose rights have not always been guaranteed and protected as the Constitution says they must be.

The Tennessee Valley Authority

One of the first times the Supreme Court used the Ninth Amendment to help them decide a case centering upon people's rights was in 1936. Yet this case, *Ashwander v. Tennessee Valley Authority*, only clarified the amendment, rather than granting specific rights that were not already named in the Constitution.

In this case, it was argued that the federal government overstepped its bounds in setting up the Tennessee Valley Authority (TVA). The TVA was developed as part of President Franklin D. Roosevelt's New Deal, a package of programs designed to end the Great Depression. The government took control of the valley's rivers, encompassing territory in Tennessee, Georgia, Alabama, Mississippi, Kentucky, North and South Carolina, Virginia, West Virginia, and Indiana.

In 1936, a legal case involving the Ninth Amendment determined that the government had not overstepped its bounds in setting up the Tennessee Valley Authority (TVA). Pictured here is the construction of the Fort Loudoun Dam in Tennessee, one of the TVA's building projects.

The TVA began flood projects that would result in the generating of hydroelectric power. This would bring electricity, modern appliances and other conveniences, and economic development to a region long mired in poverty. However, the flooding prevented citizens from accessing areas they had long used for housing, farming, and hunting. The TVA also forbade private power companies from using any of its electrical infrastructure or equipment. This prevented the power companies from competing for the right to provide electricity to valley residents and businesses.

The main question confronted by the Supreme Court in this case was: Is use of land by private individuals a right guaranteed by the Constitution, even though it is not stated directly? The Supreme Court's job was to decide if use of the Tennessee Valley was a citizen's right that could not be taken away by the government (even if that government was seizing the land in order to improve the lives and fortunes of those same citizens).

After hearing arguments from both sides and deliberating among themselves, the justices decided that the government could indeed use the land for the greater public good and that it had not abused its powers. The court explained that "the Ninth Amendment does not withdraw the rights that are expressly granted to the federal government." This means that the government's right to protect the public good—and the vulnerable people who make up the public—overrides any individual rights not expressly named in the Constitution.

The Postwar Housing Crisis

In 1948, the Ninth Amendment was again brought up in a Supreme Court case. A serious housing shortage developed in the aftermath of World War II. This shortage had two causes. The first was the large number of returning soldiers seeking places to live. The second was the supply shortage created because so many materials had been devoted to the war effort and wartime industries.

There was a danger that citizens might be taken advantage of by property owners or landlords who might overcharge for properties during this period of high housing demand and short supply. To prevent this, Congress passed the Housing and Rent Act of 1947 to help regulate prices. Even though the war had ended, Congress was still enacting wartime laws to help the country recover from problems created during the armed conflict. But did this new housing law interfere with a property owner or landlord's right to charge what he or she thought was a fair price for a house or apartment? Was the right to charge what

A legal case involving the Ninth Amendment helped determine that the Housing and Rent Act of 1947 did not interfere with the rights of property owners and landlords trying to get a fair price for their properties during the postwar housing shortage.

is deemed a fair price for goods or services a right guaranteed by the Constitution, even though this is not stated directly anywhere in it?

The Supreme Court decided again that the federal government did not overstep its bounds by enacting the Housing and Rent Act. It was agreed by the court that "war powers" included doing anything necessary "to remedy the evils which have arisen from [the war's] rise and progress." In this case, as well as in the case of the Tennessee Valley Authority, the efforts of the government to protect the interests of many citizens overrode the rights of the few individuals who might lose out because of the decision.

The Right to Participate in Politics

In a 1947 case brought before the Supreme Court, federal workers who were members of a union called the United Public Workers of America argued that their rights as American citizens were being violated. A law had been passed about ten years earlier stating that public workers were not allowed to participate in political campaigns or engage in politics in any way because they were federal government employees. When they attempted to participate in political campaigns, one worker in particular was threatened with firing. Was the right to practice politics a right guaranteed by the Constitution, though one not named directly?

In arguments before the Supreme Court, the workers claimed that the Ninth Amendment guaranteed them the right to practice politics, but the justices did not agree. They decided that the workers could not violate the law simply because they felt there was a possible threat to their unnamed personal rights. The justices also said that any rights the workers had to practice politics would have been protected under the First Amendment, which guarantees freedom of speech, not the Ninth Amendment.

How to Become a Judge

Most judges start their careers as lawyers. They obtain a degree called a Juris Doctor, or J.D. They also have to pass a test called the bar exam, which tests students' knowledge and interpretation of the laws of the state in which they intend to practice. Many cases are tried before state and federal circuit court judges. These judges are often subject to election and reelection. This forces them to do the best job they can and reduces the chances that they will issue unfair or incorrect decisions or become corrupt (by, for example, taking bribes to deliver a certain decision). The downside to elected judgeships, however, is that judges may rule based on perceived public opinion—what is popular—rather than by what the law requires. In some states, a committee appoints judges. State supreme court judges are appointed or elected depending on the rules of the individual state.

Although these first few cases involving the Ninth Amendment did not help clarify exactly which unenumerated rights were granted to American citizens, some of the uncertainty would soon come to an end.

Breaking the Law to Change the Law

It is an interesting historical fact that some of the first Ninth Amendment cases that came before the Supreme Court involved people who, in order to claim their constitutional rights, actually broke the law. In the cases involving the Housing and Rent Act of 1947 and the United Public Workers, people chose to purposely break the law because they found it to be unfair.

In the case of the Housing and Rent Act, a landlord—the Cloyd W. Miller Company—purposely raised the price of its rents 40 percent immediately after the housing law was passed. The company did this to demonstrate that it thought the law was unfair. Cloyd Miller brought the case to court, which forced a series of judges to look carefully at the law and the issues at hand. Even though the Cloyd W. Miller Company did not win its case, it brought attention to the issue and forced the government to reassess its laws.

In the case of the United Public Workers, the people involved knew they were breaking the law by taking part in political campaigns. They chose to do so anyway, knowing the possible consequences—including job loss. They felt strongly that their basic rights as American citizens were being violated by the law. By telling their side of the story to the courts, they were able to force the Supreme Court to take a close look at the law and whether it infringed on people's constitutional rights.

The United Public Workers and the Cloyd W. Miller Company didn't win their cases. Yet they brought much-needed attention to the extent of the Ninth Amendment's power to provide unenumerated constitutional rights to American citizens.

CHAPTER THREE

THE NINTH AMENDMENT AND PRIVACY ISSUES

For more than 160 years after the ratification of the Bill of Rights, the outcome of various court cases in the United States failed to identify a single unenumerated right that is guaranteed by the Ninth Amendment but not named elsewhere in the Constitution. In general, judges did not consider the amendment to be a strong or practical protection of individual citizens' rights. Many judges and lawyers found the amendment more confusing than helpful.

It was not until 1965 that the Supreme Court first heard a case that would be decided with the help of the Ninth Amendment and identify an unenumerated right. This landmark case named the right to

Estelle Griswold was the first person to really put the Ninth Amendment to the test. She stood up for the privacy rights of Planned Parenthood patients by challenging a state law banning contraception in the 1965 case *Griswold v. Connecticut*.

privacy as a fundamental, though unenumerated, right granted by the Constitution through the Ninth Amendment.

The case did not involve a person whose privacy was violated directly. The plaintiffs did not have their possessions searched and confiscated. They weren't spied upon. Their phones were not tapped. Instead, the case involved a privacy violation that was more indirect. In fact, the plaintiffs in the case were actually standing up for the privacy rights of others and the privacy of marriage. The case was *Griswold v. Connecticut*.

The Right to Privacy Is Established

In the state of Connecticut, a law banning any form of contraception, or birth control, had been on the books since 1879. However, in 1961, Dr. C. Lee Buxton and Estelle Griswold, an executive director of a family planning center in Connecticut, handed out free contraceptives to their patients. They were hoping to educate them about birth control and help families prevent unwanted pregnancies. They handed out the contraceptives for ten days before being arrested and fined $100. Instead of simply accepting their fines, Griswold and Buxton fought the case and appealed the decision to a higher court. An appeal is a request for a higher court to reconsider the ruling of a lower court.

This appeal eventually resulted in the case being reviewed by the highest court in America, the Supreme Court. The justices considered the plaintiffs' argument that it was unconstitutional to interfere with the privacy of a marriage. The plaintiffs felt that it was the exclusive right of a married couple to decide that they wished to avoid pregnancy and choose the method by which they would do so. Griswold and Buxton insisted that family planning decisions were not up to the government and that the anticontraception laws currently in place were violating people's rights.

Justice Arthur Goldberg argued in favor of citing the Ninth Amendment in the majority decision in *Griswold v. Connecticut*. This brought more attention to the amendment that was, until that time, not widely cited or respected. In fact, the Ninth Amendment had been known as the silent amendment.

A majority of Supreme Court justices agreed that privacy was indeed an important right guaranteed to American citizens and decided in favor of Griswold and Buxton. The Supreme Court discussed in great detail whether this right should be granted under the Ninth Amendment or through other amendments. Ultimately, *Griswold v. Connecticut* was settled with the help of and reference to other amendments as well.

But one judge in particular, Justice Arthur Goldberg, fought to have the Ninth Amendment cited in the majority decision. He argued that ever since the Ninth Amendment was ratified in 1791, it "has been a basic part of the Constitution which we are sworn to uphold. To hold that a right so basic and fundamental and so deep-rooted in our society as the right to privacy in marriage may be infringed because that right is not guaranteed in so many words by the first eight amendments of the Constitution is to ignore the Ninth Amendment and to give it no effect whatsoever" (as quoted by Klinkner).

Drawing Attention to the Ninth Amendment

The landmark decision in *Griswold v. Connecticut* brought national attention to the Ninth Amendment and its protection of the right to privacy. An individual's right to privacy was not a new idea. Some states had included privacy protections within their constitutions. For example, Alaska's constitution states, "The right of the people to privacy is recognized and shall not be infringed." California's says, "All people are by nature free and independent and have an inalienable right to . . . pursuing and obtaining . . . privacy." However, the U.S. Constitution provides no such explicit protection of a citizen's privacy.

The notion of privacy exists in some of the other constitutional amendments, but is not mentioned or named specifically. For example, the Third Amendment states that citizens are under no obligation to personally house American troops (this was a legacy of the Revolutionary era, when colonists were forced to provide food and shelter to British troops). The Fourth Amendment states that unreasonable searches and seizures of one's home and what is contained within it are not allowed. In large part, these amendments were added to the Constitution in order to better protect people's rights to privacy and private property.

In 1928, Supreme Court Justice Louis D. Brandeis wrote this about the idea of the right to privacy (as quoted by Klinkner):

> The makers of our Constitution undertook to secure conditions favorable to the pursuit of happiness. They recognized the significance of man's spiritual nature, of his feelings, and of his intellect. They knew that only a part of his pain, pleasure, and satisfaction of life are to be found in material things. They sought to protect Americans in their beliefs, their thoughts, their emotions, and their sensations. They conferred, as against the Government, the right to be let alone—the most comprehensive of rights and the most valued by civilized men.

As Brandeis and many other Americans saw it, the greatest protection provided by constitutionally guaranteed individual rights is the prevention of government interference in people's personal lives.

Abortion Rights

After the ruling in *Griswold v. Connecticut*, the issue of reproductive and marriage rights continued to be debated in society and fought in court. One particular privacy issue centered upon the growing concern regarding a woman's right to make her own decisions regarding reproductive rights without government interference.

What Is a Fundamental Right?

Deciding what American citizens' fundamental rights are is no easy task. Even the Supreme Court has difficulty agreeing on what should be declared a fundamental and guaranteed—though unenumerated—right under the Ninth Amendment, and what should not be. Justice Arthur Goldberg, who helped decide the landmark privacy case of *Griswold v. Connecticut*, said that Supreme Court justices "must look to the traditions and collective conscience of our people to determine whether a principle is so rooted there as to be ranked as fundamental" (as quoted by Klinkner).

Another way to determine whether or not a right is fundamental is to see if American lawmakers recognize the right. Do state laws allow or prohibit that particular right? How have lawmakers and judges in other countries viewed this supposed right? Ultimately, however, it is up to the justices of the Supreme Court to make the final decision as to what are a citizen's legal, fundamental, constitutionally protected rights.

Abortion is the deliberate ending of a pregnancy. Abortion was by no means a new issue or practice. Women around the world had been getting abortions—both legal and illegal—for hundreds of years. In fact, the biggest controversy over abortion before the twentieth century was not so much the morality or legality of the practice but the safety of the procedure. Many women—as many as one out of three—died during or after the procedure because medical technology, knowledge, and expertise were not as advanced as it is today. In addition, many women were given crude surgeries in unsafe conditions.

The first state to pass a law banning abortions was Connecticut in 1821. The main intent of the law was to protect the mother's safety. Many other states followed suit. During the late 1800s, a movement was begun to ban abortions throughout the country. Some felt the procedure was unsafe for the mother and should therefore be outlawed. Others saw abortion as a moral issue and believed that the abortion of a fetus was the taking of a life, a form of murder. The Catholic Church was an especially influential voice in the growing antiabortion movement. By 1900, abortions were banned in nearly every state.

By the 1950s, medical practices had improved to the point that abortions provided by medical doctors were much safer for women. At the same time, the role of women in society and within the family began to change. Women began to have careers outside the home and wanted to have more control over their lives. As part of this development, the issue of reproductive rights became an increasingly important concern in the United States. And a person's right to privacy was at the forefront of the fight.

Roe v. Wade

By the late 1960s, abortion was still illegal in the state of Texas. Two lawyers from Dallas named Linda Coffee and Sarah Weddington wanted to have the abortion laws overturned. To do so, they looked to Norma McCorvey. McCorvey had

Attorney Sarah Weddington (*second from left*) poses with her family and U.S. Representative George Mahon of Texas (*second from right*) on the day Weddington began arguing *Roe v. Wade* before the Supreme Court in 1971.

had a difficult life and found herself married and pregnant at the age of
sixteen. She left her husband after he beat her. She had to leave her baby
with her mother while she took a job with a traveling carnival. When
she found herself pregnant again, she knew she could not support her

new baby. Illegal abortions were unsafe in Texas, and she did not have the money to travel to another state for a safer one.

Weddington and Coffee thought McCorvey's story would help support their case for overturning the antiabortion laws when they presented it to the Texas courts. The issue of abortion had become quite controversial, and McCorvey's quickly became a high-profile case. To protect McCorvey's privacy, she was referred to as "Jane Roe" throughout the trial. The Dallas district attorney at the time was Henry Wade, and he was in charge of upholding the state's laws. So the case became known as *Roe v. Wade*.

The plaintiff's lawyers cited the earlier *Griswold v. Connecticut* Supreme Court decision in favor of privacy rights and reproductive freedom to bolster their case. They argued that Roe's right to privacy should be guaranteed by the Ninth Amendment. But this right had been violated because the government prevented her from making her own decisions about her pregnancy, body, and personal life.

The district attorney argued that a fetus is an unborn person, and, therefore, an abortion would constitute murder. He reasoned that, even if someone had a constitutionally guaranteed right to privacy, that did not mean she had the right to commit murder.

The judges in the case sided with Jane Roe. They stated that "the Texas abortion laws must be declared unconstitutional because they deprive single women and married couples of their right, secured by the Ninth Amendment, to choose whether to have children." Even though the state law was declared unconstitutional, the judges refused to issue a legal order to prohibit it. So the case had to go to the Supreme Court in order for the state law to be repealed. In the meantime, abortion was still illegal in Texas even though the judges had declared the law unconstitutional.

The Supreme Court Weighs In

As *Roe v. Wade* made its way to the Supreme Court, the issue of abortion became increasingly heated and controversial, and it remains so to this day. The Supreme Court justices heard the case beginning in late 1971. The case was re-presented in the fall of 1972 so that two newly appointed justices could hear all of the arguments from both sides.

Finally, in January 1973, the Court reached a decision. Justice Harry Blackmun wrote the Court's opinion on the case. He wrote that "the Court has recognized that a right of personal privacy, or a guarantee of certain areas or zones of privacy, does exist under the Constitution . . . This right of privacy . . . is broad enough to encompass a woman's decision whether or not to terminate her pregnancy."

The issue of abortion is very complex, and the Supreme Court's ruling took this into account. The rights of the mother had to be weighed carefully with the rights of the unborn child. The court decided that as a pregnancy progresses and the fetus becomes more viable (more able to survive outside the womb), the fetus would have more rights and the mother's health would be more endangered by a late-term abortion. Therefore, the ruling specified that states could not restrict a woman's right to an abortion during the first trimester (months one through three) of pregnancy, except to demand that it be done by a certified doctor. In the second trimester (months four through six), states could only restrict abortions to protect the health of the mother. In the third trimester (months seven through nine), the state could interfere with a woman's access to an abortion in order to protect the rights of the unborn child.

Since the *Roe v. Wade* ruling, abortion has become a fierce political, moral, and religious debate. The Supreme Court decision, far from settling the issue, seems to have fueled the debate, raised more legal questions, and hardened the battle lines. Many voters now demand that political candidates reveal their personal opinions on the issue because their legislative decisions will affect the laws of the state or country. The man or woman they vote for may someday be in a position to approve judges for state and federal courts—including the Supreme Court—who

The Supreme Court decision in *Roe v. Wade* has become so controversial that many voters want to know political candidates' position on the case before deciding whether or not to vote for them.

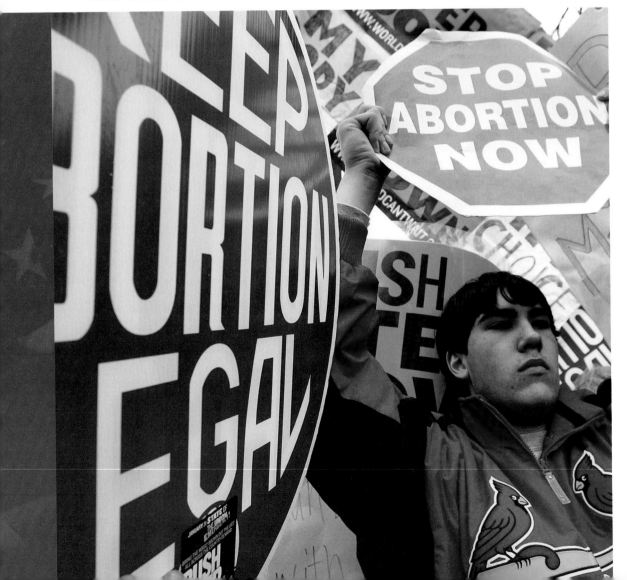

will sit in judgment of abortion challenges. State courts have grappled with difficult legal questions regarding abortion. These include whether a husband should have to be informed of his wife's intention to get an abortion and whether a minor should be required to have her parents' consent before getting an abortion.

The abortion debate ultimately boils down to a question of personal conscience and individual beliefs. But it also gets to the very heart of questions surrounding Ninth Amendment privacy protections guaranteed to every American. To what extent can the government interfere in our personal lives and decisions? When does the public good or another individual's rights trump our own? In what instances does one individual's rights trump those of another individual, and why? What are the individual rights of parents, husbands, wives, children, and the unborn, and what happens when they clash? The Ninth Amendment has placed the issue of privacy and many other important individual rights questions at the forefront of our society's most impassioned debates and discussions.

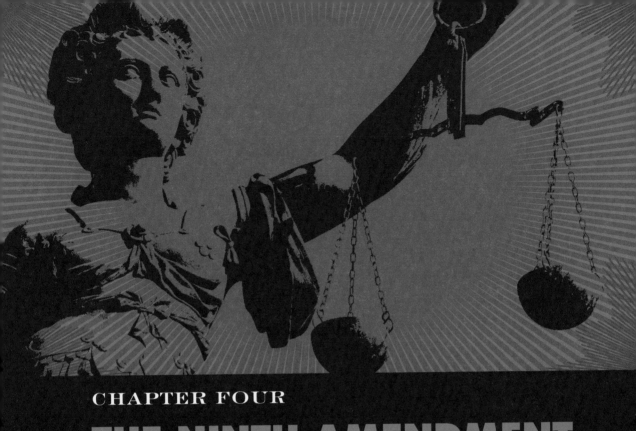

CHAPTER FOUR

THE NINTH AMENDMENT AND MODERN SOCIETY

People's attitudes about the Ninth Amendment have changed a lot over the past two centuries since it was written. The idea behind the amendment—the protection of people's rights that were not specified elsewhere in the Constitution—was important enough for the founders of our country to include it in the Bill of Rights. Yet the amendment was also vague and confusing enough that people didn't turn to it for support when attempting to defend and secure their rights in court. It is important to keep in mind that the Ninth Amendment was meant to be vague. It serves as a reminder to the government, judges, lawyers, and ordinary people that citizens have more rights than are spelled out in the Constitution. As a legal tool, it can help the courts to decide what rights should be protected by law.

Since the mid-twentieth century, the amendment has become more and more useful as an important way for people to win a guarantee of rights that they were often denied in the past. In some states, the right to privacy has been extended to cover many aspects of people's personal lives. These can range from the rights of gay and lesbian citizens to marry each other to the right of a terminally ill patient to die without extraordinary and invasive medical intervention.

The Rights of Gays and Lesbians

If the Ninth Amendment guarantees Americans' right to privacy, why isn't gay marriage legal in every state? The case in favor of legalizing gay marriage nationwide can be made by arguing that the government is interfering with the privacy of marriage, just as it did in the case of *Griswold v. Connecticut*. The problem is that some people view homosexuality as a controversial issue, just as people view abortion and contraception as controversial. Some people feel that a romantic relationship should only be between a man and a woman, and that any relationship between people of the same sex is immoral and should be considered illegal.

So who decides whether two people can get married? Is it up to the people involved, or is it up to the government that writes and enforces laws to create a fair and just society? This issue has long been debated, and it has generally been left to the individual states to decide whether to permit or forbid gay marriage.

Gay rights have been fought for in U.S. courts for a long time. While gays and lesbians have gained a lot of ground in terms of overturning

laws that discriminate against them, they still have a long way to go before they can be considered truly equal under the law. Because the Constitution does not mention the rights of gays and lesbians directly, it can be argued that they do not exist at all in the Bill of Rights. Yet,

The claims for gay marriage are based upon precedents of Ninth Amendment interpretations favoring individual rights, privacy rights, and the privacy of marriage.

like so many other Americans who insist upon certain rights not otherwise enumerated in the Constitution, the Ninth Amendment may be their best hope for obtaining full equality and fairness under the law.

The Right to Informational Privacy

Americans often feel they have a fundamental right to privacy. This includes the right to informational privacy. In the past few years, for example, laws have been overturned that demanded that employees give their private medical history to employers. These laws used to indirectly cause discrimination against employees who had an illness that necessitated time off for medical treatments or required a large amount of medical insurance payouts. People with certain conditions could lose their job or not be offered one in the first place.

These specific instances in which the laws that violated personal privacy were overturned are generally considered to be victories for fairness and justice. But what about situations in which the individual's right to privacy runs up against the general public's right to security? A person's right to privacy at an airport

is becoming a growing concern and an international one as well. In an attempt to prevent terrorist acts, air travelers are being asked to reveal more of the contents of their luggage and carry-on bags. The kinds of items they can bring onto the plane are being restricted. And

The Ninth Amendment has been cited in cases that fight to maintain the privacy of medical records. For example, employers can no longer request confidential medical information from their employees or their employees' doctors.

their bodies are being searched in ever more invasive ways, from strip searches to full-body scans and X-rays. Machines that can see under clothes are being implemented in many airports, and many people are raising the issue of privacy rights.

If legal cases questioning whether the personal privacy of travelers is compromised by reasonable security searches reach the Supreme Court, the Ninth Amendment may very well be called upon to offer guidance. It may have to help decide how to protect both a citizen's right to privacy and that same citizen's—and all of society's—right to security.

The Right to Die

Many believe that the right to die is a fundamental right that should be protected under the Ninth Amendment. When a person is terminally ill, should he or she be forced to accept medical treatment that would prolong his or her life, even if the quality of his or her life for these few extra hours, days, weeks, or months will be poor? Should a person on life support who cannot talk, think, or perform any bodily function without the help of machines be forced to stay alive just because medical technology makes it possible?

Who should be permitted to decide that a person will not ever recover and should be allowed to die a natural death? Who should be able to decide when and how life should end? These issues are very difficult ones, but they have been discussed by the Supreme Court in important cases concerning an individual's right to die.

It has been decided by the Supreme Court that a person may choose to forego life-prolonging medical treatment. But what about a patient who is in an accident and ends up in a vegetative state? This person may have no means of communication and no brain activity that reveals an awareness of his or her surroundings or situation. People in this state may be able to be kept alive indefinitely, but should they be forced to?

In the case of a Missouri woman named Nancy Beth Cruzan, severe injuries resulting from a car accident left her in an irreversible coma. She was in a vegetative state, and her quality of life had severely declined. Cruzan had no hope of recovery. Her parents tried to have her life support system removed so that she could die a natural death. But the Missouri Department of Health objected and denied their wishes.

The case went all the way to the Supreme Court. Should another person be able to make a decision regarding the withdrawal of medical treatment on a patient's behalf? The Supreme Court decided that no one else has the right to make that decision for another person. That person would have to remain on life support unless his or her end-of-life wishes were made known in writing before the accident. A person would have to formally designate someone to make those medical decisions if such a series of events came to pass.

Ultimately, friends of Cruzan came forward. They told the Court that in conversations over the years she had spoken of her desire to be

Some argue that one's medical decisions—including the decision to forego treatment of a terminal illness—are personal choices, and therefore private ones, protected by the Ninth Amendment's perceived guarantees of privacy.

removed from life support should she ever have an accident and end up in a permanent coma. As a result, the Supreme Court justices ruled in favor of the Cruzans, and the feeding tube was removed. Nancy Beth Cruzan was granted the right to die.

The Right to Travel

One fundamental right that many Americans assume they have and insist upon is the right to move freely about the country, even if only to cross town, county, or state lines. In one important case from 1969, a person who would have been entitled to welfare assistance could not receive it because he had not been a resident of the state for more than twelve months. The Supreme Court decided that the law was unconstitutional because it prevented people from living where they wished and moving about the country freely.

As a result, a person can now move from one state to another and immediately be entitled to the state benefits for which he or she is eligible and that longer-term residents enjoy. The court decided that it was "long ago recognized that the nature of our Federal Union and our constitutional concepts of personal liberty unite to require that all citizens be free to travel throughout the length and breadth of our land uninhibited by statues, rules, or regulations which unreasonably burden or restrict this movement."

If people are free to travel—and, in fact, have a fundamental right to travel—should they be

Patryce Jenkins stands below the Crescent City Connection bridge that she and many other displaced New Orleans residents were prevented from crossing to the safety of neighboring Gretna after Hurricane Katrina in 2005.

allowed to move freely within a state and not be stopped? For example, in the wake of 2005's Hurricane Katrina, storm refugees fleeing severely flooded New Orleans tried to cross a bridge into the neighboring city of Gretna. The Gretna police turned the desperate people away and closed the bridge, citing security concerns. The refugees were not allowed to escape from a dangerous situation and travel where they wished, even though their lives were in jeopardy. Did the refugees from New Orleans have a constitutional right to enter the city of Gretna? Did the Gretna police have a right to keep the peace in their community and therefore deny the strangers access?

In times of disaster or eminent danger, there is no time to take up a legal case and present it before the Supreme Court. The court systems are slow, and the Supreme Court decides cases following lengthy debates and complicated legal discussions. Whether actions taken in times of emergency were right or wrong, constitutional or unconstitutional, is usually decided months or even years later, long after the crisis has passed and the damage is done.

Yet the outcome of such cases, though they don't necessarily benefit the victims, may set a precedent to follow in future emergencies. If the Supreme Court has ruled in favor of people's right to flee a danger zone into neighboring towns and cities, lower courts will be better prepared to halt any future local attempts to restrict people's movements in times of emergency. And local police departments, aware of previous court rulings, may be less likely to turn refugees away. Perhaps they will even participate willingly in rescue and relocation efforts.

Supreme Court decisions send a clear statement to lower courts and law enforcement agencies about what people's rights are and how to uphold them. Every case decided by the court has immediate implications and future consequences for the American people.

Amendment in Action:
The Right to Education

Is the right to education a fundamental right guaranteed under the Ninth Amendment? In 1973, a Texas man named Demetrio Rodriguez was determined to find out. His children attended a school in San Antonio that had little money. He felt that his children were not getting an education that was equal to that of the children who attended wealthier San Antonio schools. Rodriguez explained that the school itself was crumbling and that falling bricks would often disrupt classes and endanger the children. There were also discipline problems that the school was not equipped to deal with because the school had little funding for staffing. He pointed out that other districts spent over $200 more per student than his district did.

A lawyer interested in the issue of equal access to education took Rodriguez's argument to the Supreme Court. Together, they argued that education is a fundamental right of all citizens, and therefore educational opportunities should be equal for all children. That meant that every district must spend an equal amount of money on each student. The state of Texas fought against Rodriguez. It claimed that there was nothing in the U.S. Constitution stating that everyone must have an equal education. It did not even state that education was a fundamental right. The state felt it was unfair to take money from wealthier districts and give it to poorer districts.

The Supreme Court voted five to four against Rodriguez. Even though the Supreme Court ruled against Rodriguez, he did not give up hope of obtaining an equal education for his children. He took his fight to the Texas Supreme Court to test whether the Texas state constitution guaranteed the right to an equal education for all students.

A careful assessment of the case revealed that the state constitution does indeed consider education a right for all Texas citizens. The system of unequal school financing had to end. Since that ruling, other states such as New Jersey, California, and Kentucky have recognized that their state constitutions also guarantee equal education—and therefore equal funding—for all of their students.

Whose Right Is It Anyway?

There have been countless cases before the Supreme Court that brought up the question of rights that are not specifically granted by the Constitution. For example, should a woman have the right to nurse in public wherever she wants? Should people have the right to bring guide dogs in places where other animals are not allowed? Should handicapped people have the right to handicapped access to any building in America? Should a child have the right to sue his or her parents for child abuse? Should a child have the right to seek government protection from an unsafe home environment? Should every citizen have a right to a college education? Should all Americans have the right to live in a radiation-free environment? Should everyone have the right to own whatever guns they choose? Should every citizen have the right to health care? Should they have the right to refuse health care if they wish?

These kinds of unanswered questions show the importance of Supreme Court decisions in our everyday lives. And they show just how difficult being a Supreme Court justice is. Weighing individual rights unspecified in the Constitution against those of the government, corporations, businesses, employers, and schools—not to mention against considerations of the public good—is an incredibly complex and difficult task. It requires a highly developed sense of fairness, balance, reasonableness, and respect for precedent.

The Ninth Amendment is no longer a "silent amendment," as it was for almost a hundred years after its ratification. It now shapes our daily lives and helps remind us that the rights stated in the Constitution are not the only rights we have.

AMENDMENTS TO THE U.S. CONSTITUTION

First Amendment (proposed 1789; ratified 1791): Freedom of religion, speech, press, assembly, and petition

Second Amendment (proposed 1789; ratified 1791): Right to bear arms

Third Amendment (proposed 1789; ratified 1791): No quartering of soldiers in private houses in times of peace

Fourth Amendment (proposed 1789; ratified 1791): Interdiction of unreasonable search and seizure; requirement of search warrants

Fifth Amendment (proposed 1789; ratified 1791): Indictments; due process; self-incrimination; double jeopardy; eminent domain

Sixth Amendment (proposed 1789; ratified 1791): Right to a fair and speedy public trial; notice of accusations; confronting one's accuser; subpoenas; right to counsel

Seventh Amendment (proposed 1789; ratified 1791): Right to a trial by jury in civil cases

Eighth Amendment (proposed 1789; ratified 1791): No excessive bail and fines; no cruel or unusual punishment

Ninth Amendment (proposed 1789; ratified 1791): Protection of unenumerated rights (rights inferred from other legal rights but that are not themselves coded or enumerated in written constitution and laws)

Tenth Amendment (proposed 1789; ratified 1791): Limits the power of the federal government

Eleventh Amendment (proposed 1794; ratified 1795): Sovereign immunity (immunity of states from suits brought by out-of-state citizens and foreigners living outside of states' borders)

Twelfth Amendment (proposed 1803; ratified 1804): Revision of presidential election procedures (electoral college)

Thirteenth Amendment (proposed 1865; ratified 1865): Abolition of slavery

Fourteenth Amendment (proposed 1866; ratified 1868): Citizenship; state due process; application of Bill of Rights to states; revision to apportionment of congressional representatives; denies public office to anyone who has rebelled against the United States

Fifteenth Amendment (proposed 1869; ratified 1870): Suffrage no longer restricted by race

Sixteenth Amendment (proposed 1909; ratified 1913): Allows federal income tax

Seventeenth Amendment (proposed 1912; ratified 1913): Direct election to the U.S. Senate by popular vote

Eighteenth Amendment (proposed 1917; ratified 1919): Prohibition of alcohol

Nineteenth Amendment (proposed 1919; ratified 1920): Women's suffrage

Twentieth Amendment (proposed 1932; ratified 1933): Term commencement for Congress (January 3) and president (January 20)

Twenty-first Amendment (proposed 1933; ratified 1933): Repeal of Eighteenth Amendment (Prohibition)

Twenty-second Amendment (proposed 1947; ratified 1951): Limits president to two terms

Twenty-third Amendment (proposed 1960; ratified 1961): Representation of District of Columbia in electoral college

Twenty-fourth Amendment (proposed 1962; ratified 1964): Prohibition of restriction of voting rights due to nonpayment of poll taxes

Twenty-fifth Amendment (proposed 1965; ratified 1967): Presidential succession

Twenty-sixth Amendment (proposed 1971; ratified 1971): Voting age of eighteen

Twenty-seventh Amendment (proposed 1789; ratified 1992): Congressional compensation

Proposed but Unratified Amendments

Congressional Apportionment Amendment (proposed 1789; still technically pending): Apportionment of U.S. representatives

Titles of Nobility Amendment (proposed 1810; still technically pending): Prohibition of titles of nobility

Corwin Amendment (proposed 1861; still technically pending though superseded by Thirteenth Amendment): Preservation of slavery

Child Labor Amendment (proposed 1924; still technically pending): Congressional power to regulate child labor

Equal Rights Amendment (proposed 1972; expired): Prohibition of inequality of men and women

District of Columbia Voting Rights Amendment (proposed 1978; expired): District of Columbia voting rights

GLOSSARY

amendment A change or addition made to a legal document.

Anti-Federalists People who opposed the granting of increased power to the federal government, and therefore also opposed the Constitution of 1787; a member of a political movement in early America who wanted states to have more power than the federal government.

appeal A request for a higher court to reconsider the ruling of a lower court.

Bill of Rights The first ten amendments to the U.S. Constitution. These amendments more clearly outline the various rights and powers of the federal government, the states, and the individual citizen.

consensus An opinion held by all or most.

curtail To cut short or reduce.

delegate A person authorized or sent to speak and act for others; a representative at a convention.

due process Fair treatment under the law.

enumerated Named, numbered, and/or specified.

Federalists People who supported the new Constitution of 1787 and the power it gave to the federal government.

fundamental Forming a foundation or basis; basic; essential; most important; relating to a principle, theory, or law serving as a basis; an essential part.

guaranteed Formally promised.

interpret To explain the meaning of; to make understandable; to bring out the meaning of; to give one's own conception of something.

precedent An earlier event, action, decision, or outcome that guides decisions in similar present and future situations.

ratify To confirm or approve something; to agree upon a proposed law and sign it.

tyranny An oppressive and unjust government; very cruel and unjust use of power or authority; harshness; severity.

unalienable Incapable of being transferred to someone else or taken away from the possessor.

unenumerated Not named, numbered, and/or specified.

vague Not clearly, precisely, or definitely expressed or stated; indefinite in shape, form, or character; hazily or indistinctly seen or sensed; not sharp, certain, or precise in thought, feeling, or expression; not precisely determined or known; uncertain.

FOR MORE INFORMATION

American Bar Association (ABA)
321 North Clark Street
Chicago, IL 60654-7598
(312) 988-5000
Web site: http://www.abanet.org
As the national representative of the legal profession, the ABA works to equally serve its members (lawyers and judges) and the public by defending liberty and delivering justice.

American Civil Liberties Union (ACLU)
125 Broad Street, 18th Floor
New York, NY 10004
(212) 549-2500
Web site: http://www.aclu.org
The ACLU views itself as the nation's guardian of liberty, working daily in courts, legislatures, and communities to defend and preserve the individual rights and liberties that the Constitution and laws of the United States guarantee every American citizen. These rights include freedom of speech, freedom of the press, freedom of association and assembly, freedom of religion, freedom from discrimination, the right to due process, and the right to privacy.

American Law Institute
4025 Chestnut Street
Philadelphia, PA 19104
(215) 243-1600
Web site: http://www.ali.org
The American Law Institute is the leading independent organization in the United States producing scholarly work to clarify, modernize, and otherwise improve the

law. The institute (made up of four thousand lawyers, judges, and law professors of the highest qualifications) drafts, discusses, revises, and publishes restatements of the law, model statutes, and principles of law that are enormously influential in the courts and legislatures, as well as in legal scholarship and education.

Harvard Law Review

Gannett House
1511 Massachusetts Avenue
Cambridge, MA 02138
(617) 495-7889
Web site: http://www.harvardlawreview.org

Aside from serving as an important academic forum for legal scholarship, the *Harvard Law Review* has two other goals. First, the journal is designed to be an effective research tool for practicing lawyers and students of the law. Second, it provides opportunities for *Review* members to develop their own editing and writing skills. The *Review* publishes articles by professors, judges, and practitioners, and solicits reviews of important recent books from recognized experts.

Legal Aid Society

199 Water Street
New York, NY 10038
(212) 577-3346
Web site: http://www.legal-aid.org

The Legal Aid Society is the nation's oldest and largest provider of legal services to those who cannot afford to hire a lawyer. Founded in 1876, the society provides a full range of civil legal services as well as criminal defense work and juvenile rights representation in family court.

National Archives and Records Administration (NARA)

8601 Adelphi Road
College Park, MD 20740-6001

Web site: http://www.archives.gov
(866) 272-6272

The NARA is the nation's record keeper. The archives house the Declaration of Independence, the Articles of Confederation, the Constitution, the Bill of Rights, the Emancipation Proclamation, and the Louisiana Purchase agreement, along with other documents of national importance like military and immigration records and even the *Apollo 11* flight plan. Archives locations in fourteen cities, from coast to coast, protect and provide public access to millions of records.

Supreme Court of the United States
1 First Street NE
Washington, DC 20543
(202) 479-3000
Web site: http://www.supremecourt.gov

The Supreme Court of the United States is the highest judicial body in the country and leads the federal judiciary. It consists of the chief justice of the United States and eight associate justices who are nominated by the president and confirmed by a majority vote of the Senate. Once appointed, justices effectively have life tenure, which terminates only upon death, resignation, retirement, or conviction on impeachment. The court meets in Washington, D.C., in the U.S. Supreme Court Building. The Supreme Court primarily hears appeals of lower court decisions.

Web Sites

Due to the changing nature of Internet links, Rosen Publishing has developed an online list of Web sites related to the subject of this book. This site is updated regularly. Please use this link to access the list:

http://www.rosenlinks.com/ausc/9th

FOR FURTHER READING

Burgan, Michael. *The Creation of the U.S. Constitution* (Graphic History). Mankato, MN: Capstone Press, 2007.

Cheney, Lynn, and Greg Harlin. *We the People: The Story of Our Constitution*. New York, NY: Simon & Schuster Children's Publishing, 2008.

Coleman, Wim, and Pat Perrin, eds. *The Constitution and the Bill of Rights*. Auburndale, MA: History Compass, 2006.

Finkelman, Paul. *American Documents: The Constitution*. Des Moines, IA: National Geographic Children's Books, 2005.

Fradin, Dennis Brindell. *The Bill of Rights* (Turning Points in U.S. History). Tarrytown, NY: Marshall Cavendish Children's Books, 2008.

Fradin, Dennis Brindell. *The Founders: The 39 Stories Behind the U.S. Constitution*. New York, NY: Walker Books for Young Readers, 2005.

Isaacs, Sally Senzell. *Understanding the Bill of Rights* (Documenting Early America). New York, NY: Crabtree Publishing Co., 2008.

JusticeLearning.org. *The United States Constitution: What It Says, What It Means: A Hip Pocket Guide*. New York, NY: Oxford University Press, 2005.

Leavitt, Amie J. *The Bill of Rights in Translation: What It Really Means*. Mankato, MN: Capstone Press, 2008.

Manatt, Kathleen G. *Law and Order*. Ann Arbor, MI: Cherry Lane Publishing, 2007.

Pederson, Charles E. *The U.S. Constitution and Bill of Rights*. Edina, MN: ABDO Publishing, 2010.

Ransom, Candice F. *Who Wrote the U.S. Constitution and Other Questions About the Constitutional Convention of 1787*. Minneapolis, MN: Lerner Classroom, 2010.

Smith, Rich. *Ninth and Tenth Amendments: The Right to More Rights*. Edina, MN: ABDO Publishing, 2007.

Sobel, Syl. *The Bill of Rights: Protecting Our Freedom Then and Now*. Hauppauge, NY: Barron's Educational Series, 2008.

Taylor-Butler, Christine. *The Bill of Rights*. New York, NY: Scholastic Library Publishing, 2008.

Taylor-Butler, Christine. *The Constitution of the United States* (True Books). New York, NY: Children's Press, 2008.

Taylor-Butler, Christine. *The Supreme Court* (True Books). New York, NY: Children's Press, 2008.

Yero, Judith Lloyd. *American Documents: The Bill of Rights*. Des Moines, IA: National Geographic Society, 2006.

BIBLIOGRAPHY

Ackerman, Bruce. *We the People, Volume 1: Foundations.* Cambridge, MA: Belknap Press, 1993.

Ackerman, Bruce. *We the People, Volume 2: Transformations.* Cambridge, MA: Belknap Press, 2000.

Amar, Akhil Reed. *America's Constitution: A Biography.* New York, NY: Random House, 2006.

Amar, Akhil Reed. *The Bill of Rights: Creation and Reconstruction.* New Haven, CT: Yale University Press, 2000.

Barnett, Randy E. *The Rights Retained by the People: The Ninth Amendment and Constitutional Interpretation.* Volume 2. Fairfax, VA: George Mason University Press, 1993.

Breyer, Stephen. *Active Liberty: Interpreting Our Democratic Constitution.* New York, NY: Vintage, 2006.

DeRosa, Marshall. *The Ninth Amendment and the Politics of Creative Jurisprudence: Disparaging the Fundamental Right of Popular Control.* Piscataway, NJ: Transaction Publishers, 1995.

Farber, Dan. *Retained by the People: The "Silent" Ninth Amendment and the Constitutional Rights Americans Don't Know They Have.* New York, NY: Basic Books, 2007.

Klinkner, Philip A. *The American Heritage History of the Bill of Rights; The Ninth Amendment.* Englewood Cliffs, NJ: Silver Burdett Press, 1991.

Kowalski, Kathiann M. *Order in the Court: A Look at the Judicial Branch.* Minneapolis, MN: Lerner Publications Company, 2004.

Lash, Kurt T. *The Lost History of the Ninth Amendment.* New York, NY: Oxford University Press, 2009.

Levinson, Sanford, ed. *Responding to Imperfection: The Theory and Practice of Constitutional Amendment.* Princeton, NJ: Princeton University Press, 1995.

Levy, Leonard W. *Origins of the Bill of Rights.* New Haven, CT: Yale University Press, 2001.

Massey, Calvin. *Silent Rights: The Ninth Amendment and the Constitution's Unenumerated Rights.* Philadelphia, PA: Temple University Press, 1995.

O'Brien, David M. *Storm Center: The Supreme Court in American Politics.* 8th ed. New York, NY: W. W. Norton & Co., 2008.

Patterson, Bennett B. *The Forgotten Ninth Amendment: A Call for Legislative and Judicial Recognition of Rights Under Social Conditions Today.* Clark, NJ: The Lawbook Exchange, Ltd., 2008.

Pendergast, Tom, Sara Pendergast, and John Sousanis. *Constitutional Amendments: From Freedom of Speech to Flag Burning.* Volume 2: Amendments 9–17. Farmington Hills, MI: The Gale Group, 2001.

Rehnquist, William H. *The Supreme Court.* New York, NY: Vintage, 2002.

Scalia, Antonin. *A Matter of Interpretation: Federal Courts and the Law.* Princeton, NJ: Princeton University Press, 1997.

Silberdick Feinberg, Barbara. *Constitutional Amendments.* Brookfield, CT: Twenty-First Century Books, 1996.

Weiss, Anne E. *The Supreme Court.* Berkeley Heights, NJ: Enslow Publishers, 1987.

Zacharias Gary, and Jared Zacharias. *The Bill of Rights.* Farmington Hills, MI: Greenhaven Press, 2003.

INDEX

A

abortion, 30–37
American Revolution, 4, 9, 30
Anti-Federalists, 10–13
Ashwander v. Tennessee Valley Authority, 18–20, 22

B

Bill of Rights, history of the, 4, 11–14
Blackmun, Harry, 35
Brandeis, Louis D., 30

C

Coffee, Linda, 32, 34
Cruzan, Nancy Beth, 44–46

E

education, the right to, 18, 49, 50

F

Federalists, 10–11, 13–14
Fifth Amendment, 16
First Amendment, 22
Fourteenth Amendment, 16
Fourth Amendment, 30
fundamental rights, determining, 31

G

gays and lesbians, rights of, 18, 39–41
Goldberg, Arthur, 29, 31
Griswold v. Connecticut, 27–29, 30, 31, 34, 39

H

Housing and Rent Act of 1947, 21–22, 23, 24

I

informational privacy, right to, 41–43

J

judge, a career as a, 23

M

Madison, James, 13
Mason, George, 11
McCorvey, Norma, 32–34

P

politics, the right to participate in, 22–23, 24
post–World War II housing crisis, 20–22
privacy, right to, 4–5, 25–30, 31–37, 39, 41–43

R

reproductive rights, 27–29, 30–37
Rodriguez, Demetrio, 49
Roe v. Wade, 32–35

S

Sedgwick, Theodore, 11
states rights vs. federal rights, 7–9
Supreme Court, overview of its role, 16–18

About the Author

Kathy Furgang has written numerous books relating to American history, government, and the law. She lives in upstate New York with her husband and two sons.

Photo Credits

Cover (left), p. 36 Alex Wong/Getty Images; cover (right) Mark Wilson/Getty Images; p. 1 (top) © www.istockphoto.com/Tom Nulens; p. 1 (bottom) © www.istockphoto.com/Lee Pettet; p. 3 © www.istockphoto.com/Nic Taylor; pp. 4–5 Comstock/Thinkstock; pp. 7, 15, 25, 38 © www.istockphoto.com/arturbo; p. 8 http://www.ourdocuments.gov; pp. 10–11 Joe Sohm/VisionsofAmerica/Getty Images; p. 13 © AP Images; pp. 16–17 www.istockphoto.com/Thinkstock; p. 19 Library of Congress Prints and Photographs Division; p. 21 H. Armstrong Roberts/Retrofile/Getty Images; p. 26 Lee Lockwood/Time & Life Pictures/Getty Images; p. 28 Joseph Scherschel/Time & Life Pictures/Getty Images; pp. 32–33 Courtesy of Sarah Weddington; pp. 40–41 David Paul Morris/Getty Images; pp. 42–43 Digital Vision/Thinkstock; p. 45 Jay Maillin/Bloomberg/Getty Images; pp. 46–47 Alex Garcia/MCT/Landov.

Photo Researcher: Amy Feinberg